WE'RE NOT CRAZY

America Has A Race Problem

WE'RE NOT CRAZY

America Has A Race Problem

REV. DR. L. RONALD DURHAM

Publisher Information:

Independently Published

P.O. Box 1773

Daytona Beach, FL. 32115

2018

United States of America

ISBN 9798504922980

The data gave in this is expressed, to be honest, and predictable, in that any risk, as far as absentmindedness or something else, by any utilization or maltreatment of any approaches, procedures, or bearings contained inside is the singular and articulate obligation of the beneficiary peruser. By no means will any lawful obligation or fault be held against the author for any reparation, harms, or money related misfortune because of the data in this, either straightforwardly or by implication.

The author claims all copyrights.

The data in this is offered for educational purposes exclusively and is all-inclusive as so. The introduction of the data is without a contract or any sort of assurance confirmation.

TABLE OF CONTENTS

Chapter 1

Slavery;

America's Original Sin

Why do Americans so easily divide into opposing groups on issues that in most other communities are settled without debate? Though social media and cable news do not help us unite, other countries' media environments are similar. Most other cultures do not approach it with the same hammer and tongs as we do.

If you watched George Floyd's last words wept onto the Minneapolis pavement, you couldn't help but be outraged or, at the very least, saddened by what appeared to be a totally unnecessary taking of a human life. Our polarization, on the other hand, took place almost instantly. African Americans saw what happened to Mr. Floyd through the lens of 400 years of oppression and a lack of caring on the part of rogue police officers. The campaign called "Defund the Police" advocated for increased funding for social care and community outreach. Others argued that the best way to bring about order was to increase law enforcement.

We have a culture war over something as innocuous as face coverings to prevent the spread of the coronavirus. (Once again, our leaders inflame the debate.) Donald Trump arguably did much to minimize the seriousness of the virus, which as a result split the nation and caused millions of Republicans to see this crisis as only a political issue used to oppose Democrats who trust the science. On the other hand, some nations have misguided leaders without the same result.) Whether we like it or not, we're living inside Dr. Suess's fable about star-bellied sneetches shunning all without a green star, and vice versa.

Our ludicrous face-mask face-off and the new Black Lives Matter campaign have more in common than you would expect. It's past time for the United States of America to face its original sin. The ending should be obvious from the name alone.

Our country has struggled for nearly four centuries to come to terms with its legacy of slavery and genocide. Slavery has been dubbed "America's Original Sin." The first slave ship landed in America in 1619, but something far worse had already arrived.

Puritans had already found themselves in Jamestown, with no grand aspirations other than religious liberty. They mostly desired to be left alone to live their lives as they saw fit. Native Americans who were already here when Europeans arrived, were not willing to be converted to a formal form of Christianity.

Many indigenous peoples were killed. Others were ostracized. All of them were scorned. Puritans generally refused to accept African slaves when they arrived later. Those who purchased slaves took pride in treating them differently than their non-slave-owning neighbors. Slavery was just the beginning of Americans' sneeze-like instinct to divide our fragile democracy into "us" and "them."

Depending on the place and time during the years of African American enslavement the treatment by slave owners was brutal. Multiple beatings with whips, and systematic rapes of women were commonplace occurrences. Most often these brutalities were done on plantations outside the view of outsiders, or even out of the sight of the slave owners' immediate family. If you were a slave you had few if any rights granted to you by whites. Testifying against a white person in a court of law was not permitted. Often a slave would be required by his master to beat other slaves, including members of their own family.

It was a common practice to spilt families by selling off children, or the man in the household, and they may not ever see their family members again. It was rare but occasionally you might find a white slave owner who treated his slaves with a measure of dignity. That could change in a heartbeat however if that plantation owners died and someone became master. No matter how nice a slave may have been treated, freedom was always in the back of their minds.

Slavery was a horrible experience. The sanctimony was — and continues to be — far worse.

Everyone in America is a better person than thou. It's just that everybody is suspicious of a certain "thou" than whom they consider themselves superior. It isn't just about police budgets and public health plans. It's everything. Did you carry your own shopping bag, and did the person in the grocery line ahead of you do the same? We can't help but pay attention.

Is your next-door neighbor an electric car driver, or do they insist on buying American? Or do they justify their SUV based on their children's safety? Is driving evidence that they lack the moral fiber woven into your carbon fiber bicycle frame?

Are you an Amazon shopper looking to save money or cut down on driving distance? Is it more important to help local businesses than convenience and variety? Do you have white or brown eggs in your refrigerator? I'm guessing you buy the same color every time because you think they (and yourself) are better.

We're still on the lookout for those we consider to be second-class citizens. We've all been enslaved by this sanctimonious habit.

The white race's legacy

The United States of America was created as a white society built on the partial genocide of one race and the subsequent enslavement of another.

Today, making such a comment is met with accusations of being bombastic or, worse, "reminiscent of the 1960s." The answer is both instructive and revelatory. The historical record of white Europeans conquering North America by eradicating the indigenous people and then building their new nation's economy on the backs of captured Africans who had been converted into chattel is hard to dispute. However, to talk frankly about such historical evidence, one risks being accused of being polemical or out of date. What is the reason for this?

One explanation for this is that racism is no longer a contentious issue. Following the brief "racial crisis" of the 1960s, white America, including many civil rights activists, has moved on to other issues.

Furthermore, most white Americans believe that the legal victories of African Americans during that period have resolved the question, prompting many to ask, "What more do blacks want?"

Civil rights law, which was intended to address discrimination against African Americans, has been interpreted by federal courts to refer to whites who think affirmative action policies have "gone too far." Furthermore, common racial views have shifted, as shown by opinion polling and the increased presence of black faces in sports, entertainment, the media, and even politics.

Many things have changed, and some haven't in the four decades since landmark civil rights legislation was passed. What has changed are many white Americans' personal, racial views and the opportunities for some African Americans to rise to the middle ranks of society. (The word "middle" is important here since African Americans are still barred from most of the top echelons and decision-making positions in business, the professions, the media, and even sports and entertainment, where black "progress" is often celebrated.) With the extension of social interchange and voting rights, legal segregation has been taken off the backs of African Americans, resulting in shifts in white attitudes.

What has not changed is the systemic and prevalent nature of racism in the United States and the majority of African Americans' living conditions. In reality, the situation in many instances has deteriorated.

Racism arises from dominance and offers the social rationale and moral justification for dehumanizing, exploiting, and harming individuals based on their skin color. Racism is sustained by both personal perceptions and systemic forces, as many have pointed out. Racism may be overtly violent, institutionalized, or both. Its spectrum encompasses all aspects of human psychology, society, and culture. While prejudice is a fundamental human sin, racism is more than a byproduct of human existence or a social accident. On the other hand, racism is an oppressive mechanism that targets a group of people who share certain defining characteristics, such as skin color or faith. This system is upheld by favorable and unfavorable rules, policies, and views that determine which community in society has fewer chances for success and happiness.

Slavery was abolished in America on December 6, 1865, when the 13th Amendment to the Constitution was ratified. That is a reality, not the opinion of a political pundit specializing in blue-state economics. On December 6, 1865 America's original sin was formally documented in our Constitution, and there should be no question about it.

...With the exception that racism still persists today...

CHAPTER 2

CIVIL WAR ENDS, JIM CROW BEGINS

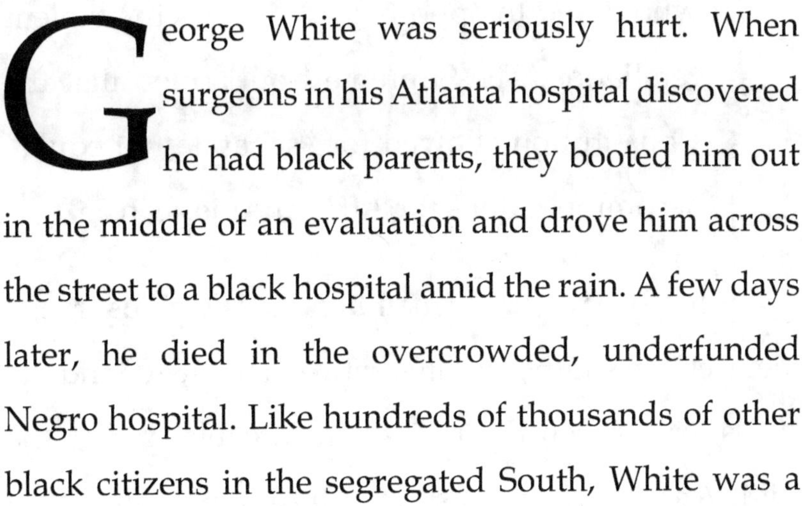

George White was seriously hurt. When surgeons in his Atlanta hospital discovered he had black parents, they booted him out in the middle of an evaluation and drove him across the street to a black hospital amid the rain. A few days later, he died in the overcrowded, underfunded Negro hospital. Like hundreds of thousands of other black citizens in the segregated South, White was a victim of Jim Crow segregation laws in the year 1931.

OVERVIEW

» From the 1870s to the 1960s, white southerners developed Jim Crow laws to impose racial segregation across the South.

» "Water fountains, public schools, bus waiting areas, movie theaters, swimming pools, and restrooms all had "whites only" and "colored" signs.

» The Supreme Court ruled Jim Crow segregation legal in the Plessy v. Ferguson decision in 1896, putting African Americans who dared to oppose it in jail or facing violent retaliation. The Supreme Court ruled that the Constitution allowed for "separate but equal" accommodations for African Americans.

Jim Crow laws maintained a vicious racial hierarchy in southern states between the 1870s and the 1960s, circumventing rights put into place after the Civil War ended, such as the 15th Amendment, which granted black men the right to vote 150 years ago.

Discriminatory laws deprived black people of their rights, humiliated them in public, and marginalized them economically and educationally. Anyone who dared to question the social order was subjected to ridicule, violence, and even murder.

The word "Jim Crow" dates back to the 1820s when white comedian Thomas Rice created the character. The stereotypical character became a stock character in minstrel shows and a common nickname for black people.

The 13th Amendment officially abolished slavery in the United States after the Civil War ended. White residents of the former Confederacy, on the other hand, opposed emancipation and moved rapidly to deny black people their newfound liberties. They enacted "black codes" that denied black people anything from land ownership, to free movement, to business ownership, using former slave laws as a model. The codes were "intended to produce a near approximation of the now forbidden master-slave relationship," according to historian Daniel A. Novak.

In reaction to the northern outcry over the codes, Congress passed constitutional amendments known as the Reconstruction Amendments, which guaranteed formerly enslaved people's freedom and civil rights. The 14th Amendment ensured citizenship and equal treatment under the law, while the 15th Amendment prohibited voting rights discrimination based on "race, color, or previous state of servitude."

To be readmitted to the Union, Southern states had to ratify the amendments. On the other hand, states grudgingly followed federal legislation while undoing as few black codes as possible. Meanwhile, organizations such as the Ku Klux Klan terrorized and murdered black people who dared to question the now-unwritten rules of conduct.

The historian Elaine Frantz Parsons describes the membership:

"Lifting the Klan mask revealed a chaotic multitude of antiblack vigilante groups, disgruntled poor white farmers, wartime guerrilla bands, displaced Democratic politicians, illegal whiskey distillers, coercive moral reformers, sadists, rapists, white workmen fearful of black competition, employers trying to enforce labor discipline, common thieves, neighbors with decades-old grudges, and even a few freedmen and white Republicans who allied with Democratic whites or had criminal agendas of their own. Indeed, all they had in common, besides being overwhelmingly white, southern, and Democrats, was that they called themselves, or were called, Klansmen." (From Wikipedia.org)

Rutherford B. Hayes, the new president, kept his pledge to end federal interference in the South in 1877. Southern states quickly repealed Reconstruction-era laws and replaced them with new segregation laws. The floodgates opened after the Supreme Court ruled in Plessy v. Ferguson in 1896 that "separate but equal" facilities were legal. Hundreds of legislations were enacted in Southern states mandating different treatment for black and white people.

Though the legislation theoretically promised black people equality, the truth was far from it. Black people were required to use different facilities that were substandard and in bad repair. Interaction between black and white people was practically prohibited. Despite the 15th Amendment's protections, Jim Crow used taxes, literacy tests, and all-white primaries to keep black people out of the polls.

These laws came to govern every aspect of southern life, establishing what historian Douglas A. Blackmon has named "slavery by another name." They were upheld by racist law enforcement and lynching. The "separate but equal" law would not be declared unconstitutional until after Brown v. Board of Education in 1954. Overt Jim Crow laws were finally repealed a decade later by the Civil Rights Act of 1964 and the Voting Rights Act of 1965. However, even though the laws are no longer in place, their consequences continue to reverberate, and existing patterns of racial profiling in law enforcement and other social arenas have echoes of Jim Crow.

"Jim Crow" has long been a degrading slang word for a black man, so the laws that were in effect in the South and some border states from 1877 to the mid-1960s were appropriately named. These laws were put in place after the Civil War to keep racial segregation in place. Jim Crow laws allowed white people and people of color to be separated on all types of public transit and in schools initially. Segregation eventually spread to colleges, cemeteries, parks, theaters, and restaurants, including contact and mixing. Anyone accused of having a black ancestor, even though it was a long time ago, was often considered an individual of color and therefore subject to Jim Crow rules. The overarching goal of Jim

Crow laws was to keep black and white people from interacting as equals, thus elevating white people above black people.

When the Supreme Court ruled in 1877 that states couldn't ban segregation on popular modes of transportation like trains, streetcars, and riverboats, Jim Crow laws were established. Later, in 1883, the Supreme Court struck down portions of the Civil Rights Act of 1875, reaffirming the principle of "separate but equal." In the years that followed, states passed legislation requiring separate and fair accommodations for blacks on public transportation. Separate schools, hospitals, churches, cemeteries, restrooms, and jails were often provided for black people. These services were mostly inferior to those provided for white people, despite the regulations requiring that the separate facilities be of comparable standard. Jim Crow laws have had an impact on how blacks and whites interacted socially. Fines or imprisonment were imposed if these laws were not enforced.

Jim Crow laws continued to regulate daily life in America well into the twentieth century, banning black and white contact. In Georgia, for example, blacks and whites were required to use different parks. A 1930 law prohibited blacks and whites from playing checkers together in Birmingham, Alabama. In Oklahoma, blacks and whites were prohibited from boating together in 1935. When blacks broke these rules, they could be violently beaten by whites without fear of retaliation; lynching's were common when blacks broke Jim Crow laws.

When World War II began, and the United States joined the fight, Jim Crow laws were still in place. In certain parts of the nation, racial segregation was a way of life, so black men serving in the military were assigned to segregated units. Black servicemen were transferred to lower-level support jobs such as gravedigging or cooking, and their meals were served in different lines from those of white servicemen. Initially, black servicemen were not allowed to fight, but as the war progressed, an increasing number of them were assigned to front-line positions, where they excelled.

One such notable group of African American servicemen in World War II were the vaunted Tuskegee Airmen. They began their training at the Tuskegee Airfield in Alabama. They became the first all-Black flying unit in the U.S. military. Both the NAACP as well as members of the Black press urged the formation of an African American unit to be trained as pilots. There was some disappointment when President Franklin D. Roosevelt decided to these would be separate all Black units thereby perpetuating segregation and discrimination. Nevertheless, the Tuskegee Airmen were born and Lieutenant Colonel Benjamin Oliver Davis Jr., became squadron's commander.

Their first mission was a strafing run on Pantelleria Island on the coast of the Mediterranean Sea. They fought extensively in the European theater and were notably one of the Air Forces' most decorated escort group units.

Altogether there were 922 pilots who graduated from the training courses at the Tuskegee Air Field, and they flew a combined total of 1,578 missions and 15,553 sorties, they also destroyed 261 enemy aircraft, and won more than 850 medals.

Following the conclusion of WWII, America's segregation practices were scrutinized. President Harry Truman formed a commission to investigate the situation, and in 1948, he signed an executive order banning racial discrimination in all branches of the military. With a string of Supreme Court wins for civil rights in the ensuing years, the tide started to turn noticeably toward equality. The Civil Rights Act, which rendered Jim Crow laws obsolete, marked the culmination of this movement, with black people steadily breaking down racial barriers and successfully resisting segregation. This law made discrimination in any kind of public accommodation illegal. The Voting Rights Act of 1965 was passed to protect black people's right to vote by banning discriminatory voting laws.

Jim Crow: a sign of racial discrimination.

Jim Crow racism was a way of life characterized by anti-black legislation and racially biased cultural traditions. In the United States, the word "Jim Crow" is often used to refer to racial segregation, especially in the South. From the 1870s to the 1960s, the Jim Crow South was when local and state legislation imposed legal segregation between white and black residents. It was illegal for black people to travel in the front of public buses, eat at a "whites only" diner, or attend a "white" public school in the Jim Crow South.

Jim Crow also had a more subtle social component, requiring African Americans to show their inferiority and subservience to whites constantly. If a black man succeeded in business, his store could be set on fire by envious whites. A black woman who refused to move off the sidewalk to make room for a white man could be fired the next day by her employer. A black man seen with a white woman might be hanged in the center of town. Any assertion of pride or equality by African Americans was regarded as an insult by most Southern whites.

One of the most notable incidents of pure hatred was that of Emmett Louis Till.

Emmett Till was born in the city of Chicago on July 25, 1941. At age 14 he took what would become a fateful trip to visit with relatives in rural Mississippi. Prior to leaving his home his mother had warned him about behaving himself while he was there. She knew full well how whites would expect a young black boy to act, and Emmett was accustomed to being a little bit of a jokester. In Chicago that would be tolerated, but his mother knew that down south it could be trouble.

Emmett arrived in the small town of Money, Mississippi, on August 21, 1955 and stayed with his great-uncle, Moses Wright, who was a local sharecropper, and Emmett spent his days helping the family with the cotton harvest. On August 24, Emmett and some of his teenage relatives went to a local grocery store after work.

At this point there are several accounts of what actually happened. There is a report of a dare for Emmett to talk with a white woman named Carolyn Bryant, who was the cashier in the store. It was then reported that Emmett whistled at, or touched the waist or hand of, or perhaps may have flirted with Carolyn before they left the store. But whatever may happened no one told his great-uncle of the incident once they got home. It was early in the morning of August 28, that Roy Bryant, the husband of Carolyn, along with his half-brother J.W. Milam, literally broke into the home of Mr. Wright and abducted Emmett at gunpoint. Both Bryant and Milam severely beat

Emmett, to the point of gouging out one of his eyes. After beating him they took him down to the Tallahatchie River. Once there they killed him with a shot to the head, tied his body to a large metal fan with barbed wire and then dumped his dead body into the river.

Emmett's uncle Mr. Wright reported the kidnapping to the police the next day and Wright and Milam were arrested. It wasn't until August 31, 1955 that they found the body of Emmett in the river. Because of their brutality his face was unrecognizable, and they were only able to identify him because he was wearing a monogrammed ring that belonged to his father. Less than 2 weeks after heading south, on September 2 the train bearing his body arrived back in Chicago. In one of the most provocative statements of courage his mother choose to keep the casket of her son open during the funeral, so that the whole nation could see the brutality of these white men on an innocent 14 year boy. The riveting images of his tortured body were published in the pages of Jet magazine and the Chicago Defender, and his murder became one of the lynchpins of the civil rights movement.

Bryant and Milam were found not guilty by an all-white all male jury (at that time Black were not allowed to serve as jurors in Mississippi). Both men were later paid to tell their story of the kidnapping and murder in a 1956 article that appeared in Look magazine. Because of the double jeopardy statues they could not be retried.

In 2004 the F.B.I. did reopen the case. By that time Bryant and Milam were both dead, but agents sought to retrace the final hours of Emmett's life. It was an exhaustive three year investigation that included exhuming the body of Emmett and doing a complete autopsy. There were not charges filed but Milam's brother Leslie on his deathbed did confess to his own involvement in the kidnapping and murder.

After the body was exhumed Emmett was buried in a new casket and his original one was later found rusting and abandoned in a work shed on the back of the Burr Oak Cemetery property. Later however Emmett's original casket was donated to the Smithsonian's National Museum of African American History and Culture.

Since the late 1800s, the term Jim Crow has been used to describe the social and legal separation between black and white Americans. Following the Civil War and Reconstruction, whites disenfranchised black men (through poll taxes, literacy tests, and other means), reduced black workers to low-paying jobs, and underfunded black public schools. Whites in the Jim Crow South created a bitter network of political, economic, and social barriers to full and equal citizenship for their black neighbors in this way.

Plessy v. Ferguson and the civil rights movement.

Rosa Parks was not the first to speak out about segregated public transit. Homer Plessy, an African American man from New Orleans, had questioned segregated rail cars more than fifty years before. Plessy was arrested in 1892 when he boarded a train in a "whites-only" compartment and refused to transfer to a "colored" compartment when asked. (Plessy intended to be imprisoned to challenge Louisiana's segregation statute, claiming that it violated the Fourteenth Amendment's guarantee of equal protection under the law for all citizens.)

Plessy's anti-segregation lawsuit made its way through the courts before it reached the Supreme Court in 1896. The Supreme Court decided in a plurality opinion that Louisiana's segregation law did not violate the Fourteenth Amendment because separate housing for whites and blacks were equal.

Justice Henry Brown summarized the majority decision as follows: "The plaintiff's fundamental fallacy, we believe, is the belief that the forced division of the two races imbues the colored race with a stigma of inferiority. If this is true, it is not because of something contained in the act, but because the colored race has chosen to create it in that way."

The Plessy decision made racial discrimination legal in the country. While Jim Crow segregation was most virulent in the Deep South, some segregationist practices existed throughout the United States, particularly in housing, banking, and employment.

The end of Jim Crow segregation came under increasing attack after World War II. When he joined the Brooklyn Dodgers in 1947, Jackie Robinson broke baseball's color barrier. President Harry S. Truman signed an executive order desegregating the US military in 1948.

The Plessy decision was not reversed until 1954 when the Supreme Court ruled that segregated facilities were "inherently unequal" in Brown v. Board of Education of Topeka. Via legislation that rendered it illegal to segregate public buildings, restrict voting, discriminate in housing, or ban interracial marriage, Jim Crow was gradually dismantled in the 1960s due to the Civil Rights Movement's efforts.

CHAPTER 3

SYSTEMIC RACISM IS INGRAINED IN THE CULTURE

In American establishments, racial, monetary, housing, and educational inequalities are deeply entrenched. Even though the Declaration of Independence states that "all men are created equal," the American vote-based system has consistently avoided such controversy. In 2017, Harry Rubenstein, the caretaker of the National Museum of American History, said, "The majority rules system means anyone can participate; it means you're imparting capacity to people you don't know, don't understand, and probably won't care about." That is the agreement. Furthermore, a few people have felt undermined by that thinking over time.

Disparities vary from the obvious to less blatant structures and conviction systems. Survey burdens that sufficiently disappointed African American voters; the depreciation of African American fighters who fought in World War I and World War II but were treated as peons at home; black trailblazers who were barred from documenting their developments; white clinical experts' abuse of people of color's bodies.

Accounts posted by black children are among the most tragic examples of auxiliary prejudice's direct impact. During a trip to the Connecticut shore in the late 1970s, Lebert F. Lester II, then 8 or 9 years old, started constructing a sandcastle. A young white young lady accompanied him, but her father removed her right away. "For what cause don't [you] simply go in the water and wash it off?" Lester inquired of the young lady who had returned. "I was so befuddled," Lester says, "I only made sense of it later when she implied my composition."

Minnijean Brown, then 15 years old, had arrived at Little Rock Central High School in 1957 with high hopes of "making friends, going to plays, and singing in the chorale." Instead, she and the other Little Rock Nine—a group of black students who wanted to attend an earlier all-white school after Brown v. Board of Education integrated state-funded schools—were subjected to daily verbal and physical assaults. Around the same time, photographer John G. Zimmerman captured glimpses of racial legislative problems in the South, including black families waiting in long lines for polio vaccines while white children received prompt care.

The Kerner Commission, convened by President Lyndon B. Johnson in 1968, concluded that white prejudice, not black anger, was the guiding force behind the country's unending common chaos. "Bad police policies, an imperfect equity system, crooked shopper credit practices, unsafe or deficient lodging, high joblessness, voter concealment, and other socially installed forms of racial discrimination all joined in impelling brutal reform," wrote Alice George in 2018. Few people were aware of the findings, let alone its call for aggressive government spending to even the odds. Rather, the country realized another reason: space travel. The biggest black paper in New York, the New York Amsterdam News, published a story the day after the 1969 moon landing, expressing, "The moon was there yesterday. Maybe it'll be us tomorrow."

A different study released fifty years after the Kerner Report's release looked at how much had changed and concluded that conditions had worsened. In 2017, both the rate of detained black people and the rate of black joblessness were higher than in 1968. The wealth gap had also widened significantly, with a middle-class white family having multiple times the wealth of a middle class black family. "We are desegregating our urban neighborhoods and our schools, sentenced a great many children to second-rate schooling and eliminating their legitimate chance of escaping poverty," Fred Harris, the last surviving member of the Kerner Commission, said after the report's release in 2018.

Despite overwhelming evidence that race has only social, not organic, meanings, local bigotry persists, based on such flawed practices as genetic counseling and the treatment of race "as a rough intermediary for horde social and ecological variables," as Ramin Skibba puts it. Black scholars like Mamie Phipps Clark, a psychiatrist whose study of racial character in children helped end school alienation, and Rebecca J. Cole, a nineteenth-century doctor, and supporter who proved that black networks were doomed to death and disease, have helped to dispel some of these notions.

Regardless, a 2015 study found that 48 percent of black and Latina women, respectively, report being confused with custodial or regulatory workers. Indeed, even artificial reasoning reveals racial biases, many of which are presented by lab workers and publicly funded experts who program their own conscious and oblivious analyses into calculations.

From the Britanica.com: "In their work *Critical Race Theory: An Introduction*, first published in 2001, the legal scholars Richard Delgado (one of the founders of CRT) and Jean Stefancic discuss several general propositions that they claim would be accepted by many critical race theorists, despite the considerable variation of belief among members of the movement. These "basic tenets" of CRT, according to the authors, include the following claims:

(1) Race is socially constructed, not biologically natural.

(2) Racism in the United States is normal, not aberrational: it is the common, ordinary experience of most people of color.

(3) Owing to what critical race theorists call "interest convergence" or "material determinism," legal advances (or setbacks) for people of color tend to serve the interests of dominant white groups. Thus, the racial hierarchy that characterizes American society may be unaffected or even reinforced by ostensible improvements in the legal status of oppressed or exploited people.

(4) Members of minority groups periodically undergo "differential racialization," or the attribution to them of varying sets of negative stereotypes, again depending on the needs or interests of whites.

(5) According to the thesis of "intersectionality" or "antiessentialism," no individual can be adequately identified by membership in a single

group. An African American person, for example, may also identify as a woman, a lesbian, a feminist, a Christian, and so on. Finally, (

(6) the "voice of color" thesis holds that people of color are uniquely qualified to speak on behalf of other members of their group (or groups) regarding the forms and effects of racism. This consensus has led to the growth of the "legal story telling" movement, which argues that the self-expressed views of victims of racism and other forms of oppression provide essential insight into the nature of the legal system." **(Britanica.com)**

CHAPTER 4

FROM SLAVE CATCHERS TO POLICE OFFICERS; A RACIST HISTORY

The Origins of American Policing and a Brief History of Slavery

The origins and evolution of the American police force can be traced back to various historical, legal, and political-economic factors. Slavery and the domination of minorities, on the other hand, were two of the most powerful historical aspects of American society that shaped early policing. Slave patrols and Night Watches, which evolved into modern police forces, were both created to keep minorities in check. For example, Indian Constables were assigned to police Native Americans in New England (National Constable Association, 1995), the St. Louis police department was created to protect people from Native Americans in that frontier area, and several southern police forces started primarily as slave patrols. The first slave patrol in the United States was established in 1704 in the colony of Carolina. Slave patrols aided wealthy landowners in recovering and punishing slaves who were effectively considered property, as well as maintaining economic order.

Slavery was not the only social system entangled with policing. Through legislation passed at both the state and national levels of government, slavery was completely institutionalized in the American economic and legal order. Between 1689 and 1865, Virginia, for example, passed more than 130 slave laws. Contrary to people's belief, slavery and the abuse of people of color were not just a southern issue. Laws were passed in Connecticut, New York, and other colonies to criminalize and govern slaves. In 1793 and 1850, Congress passed fugitive slave laws, which allowed for the capture and return of fugitive slaves. "The literature clearly shows that a legally sanctioned law enforcement scheme existed in America before the Civil War for the express purpose of regulating the slave population and defending the rights of slave owners," writes Turner, Giacopassi, and Vandiver (2006:186). The parallels between slave patrols and contemporary American policing are far too striking to overlook. As a result, the slave patrol is a forerunner to modern American law enforcement."

Slavery and prejudice were not abolished after the Civil War. Indeed, it was obvious that the anti-Reconstruction vigilante groups exacerbated extreme violence against people of color. Since vigilantes had no external constraints by definition, lynch mobs had a well-deserved reputation for hanging minorities first and asking questions later. Long after the Civil War, America had a long and shameful history of mistreating people of color due to its slavery legacy, which was based on the racial rationalization that Blacks were subhuman. The Ku Klux Klan, founded in the 1860s and is perhaps the most well-known American vigilante group, was notorious for assaulting and lynching Black men for transgressions that would not be considered crimes at all if committed by a White man. Lynchings took place all over the country, not just in the South. In 1871, Congress finally passed the Ku Klux Klan Act, prohibiting state actors from infringing on the civil rights of all people, in part due to law enforcements involvement with the notorious party. However, despite the passage of this law, racial and ethnic violence continued well into the 1960s.

While having white skin did not protect ethnic minorities such as the Irish or Italians from prejudice in America, it did make it easier for them to integrate into the mainstream. For those with black, brown, red, or yellow skin, the added stigma of racism has made the transformation even more difficult. Black people have long been targets of violence, in part due to the legacy of slavery.

One of the forerunners of formal police forces, particularly in the South, was the use of patrols to apprehend runaway slaves. Even after the passage of the Civil Rights Act of 1964, this disastrous legacy remained a part of the police role. In some cases, police harassment actually meant that people of African origin were more likely to be stopped and questioned by the cops, while at the other end of the spectrum, they have been beaten and even killed by White cops. The shockingly high number of people of African origin killed, beaten, and detained by police in major American cities continues to raise questions.

The term "driving while black" is in direct correlation to often common practice of singling out a motorist for harassment because of the color of their skin. In fact there are very few black people who will not tell you they have been stopped, or had a family member stopped by white police officers on a regular basis. These practices have caused tremendous distrust of the police in the black community.

It would be easy to believe that the police officer has been around since the dawn of humanity. That is the sentiment expressed in President John F. Kennedy's announcement designating the week of May 15 as "National Police Week," in which he said that law enforcement officers have been protecting Americans since the country's founding.

According to Gary Potter, a crime historian at Eastern Kentucky University, the United States police force is a relatively recent development, fueled by shifting notions of public order, which are influenced in turn by economics and politics.

Colonial America's policing had been very informal, relying on a for-profit, privately financed scheme that hired people on a part-time basis. Volunteers signed up for a specific day and time to look out for fellow colonists engaged in prostitution or gambling, a common practice in most towns. (One was founded in Boston in 1636, New York in 1658, and Philadelphia in 1700.) However, the system was inefficient since watchmen often slept and drank while on duty, and some people were assigned to watch duty as a means of punishment.

Constables supervised night-watch staff, but it wasn't necessarily a common task. According to Potter, early police officers "didn't want to wear uniforms because these guys had poor reputations, to begin with, and they didn't want to be known as people that other people didn't like." "If you were wealthy enough, you paid someone to do it for you — ironically, a thief or a neighborhood thug" when localities tried compulsory service.

However, as the country expanded, various areas used different police systems.

Increased urbanization made the night-watch system entirely obsolete in towns, as populations grew too large. In Boston, the first publicly funded, organized police force with full-time officers was founded in 1838. According to Potter, Boston was a major shipping commercial hub, and companies had been recruiting people to protect their property and ensure the secure transport of goods from the port to other locations. These businessmen devised a method of saving money by passing the expense of maintaining a police force to residents, claiming that it was for the "common good."

The economics that drove the development of police forces in the South, on the other hand, was focused on the preservation of slavery rather than the security of shipping interests. Slave patrols, which were charged with tracking down runaways and preventing slave revolts, were among the most important policing organizations, according to Potter; the first organized slave patrol was established in the Carolina colonies in 1704. During the Civil War, the military became the dominant form of law enforcement in the South. Still, during Reconstruction, many local sheriffs acted similarly to slave patrols, enforcing segregation and disenfranchisement of freed slaves.

Throughout the 19th century and beyond, the concept of public order — which the police officer was responsible for upholding — varied depending on who was asked.

For example, late-nineteenth-century businessmen had political contacts and a mental picture of the types of individuals most likely to strike and disrupt their workforce. Fears of labor union organizers and large waves of Catholic, Irish, Italian, German, and Eastern European immigrants, who looked and acted differently from those who had previously dominated cities, drove the call for the preservation of law and order, or at least the version promoted by dominant interest. e.g., Others may have seen people who drank in taverns rather than at home as "dangerous," but they should have pointed out other factors, such as how living in a smaller home makes drinking in a tavern more appealing. (As Potter points out, the hypocrisy of this argument is that the businessmen who held this view were frequently the ones who profited from the commercial selling of alcohol in public places.)

At the same time, since the late nineteenth century was the age of political machines, police captains and sergeants for each precinct were often chosen by the local political party ward chief, who also owned taverns or managed street gangs that intimidated voters. They might then use the police to threaten political enemies or pay officers to turn a blind eye to underage drinking, gambling, and prostitution.

During Prohibition, this situation became even worse, prompting President Hoover to appoint the Wickersham Commission in 1929 to investigate the ineffectiveness of law enforcement around the country. The map of police precincts was updated so that they did not align with political wards to make police independent of political party ward leaders.

Following that came the push to professionalize the police, which means that the idea of a career cop as we know it today is less than a century old.

Chapter 5

Be Not Deceived, The Civil Right Act Didn't End Racism

Civil Rights Act of 1964

The Civil Rights Act of 1964, which was meant to abolish segregation in public places and prohibit job discrimination based on race, color, religion, sex, or national origin, is regarded as one of the civil rights movement's crowning legislative achievements. President John F. Kennedy proposed it, and it overcame stiff resistance from southern members of Congress before being signed into law by Kennedy's successor, Lyndon B. Johnson. Congress extended the act in subsequent years, passing new civil rights legislation such as the Voting Rights Act of 1965.

The era preceding the Civil Rights Act of 1964

Following the Civil War, a trio of constitutional amendments abolished slavery (the 13 Amendment), granted citizenship to formerly enslaved people (the 14 Amendment), and guaranteed the right to vote to all men regardless of race (the 15 Amendment).

Nonetheless, several states, especially in the South, used poll taxes, literacy tests, and other measures to disenfranchise African Americans effectively. They also imposed rigid segregation by "Jim Crow" laws and supported white nationalist groups like the Ku Klux Klan in their acts of violence.

The United States Congress did not pass a single civil rights act for decades after Reconstruction. Finally, in 1957, the Justice Department created a civil rights division and a Commission on Civil Rights to examine unequal conditions.

Three years later, Congress established a system of court-appointed referees to assist African Americans in registering to vote. To counter southern opposition, both of these bills were heavily watered down.

When John F. Kennedy first took office in 1961, he was hesitant to embrace new anti-discrimination legislation. But, with demonstrations erupting throughout the South, including one in Birmingham, Alabama, where police used dogs, clubs, and high-pressure fire hoses to suppress unarmed protesters violently, Kennedy decided to take action.

He introduced the most comprehensive civil rights legislation to date in June 1963, stating that the

US "will not be completely free until all of its people are free."

The civil right act didn't end racism

Less than half of white Americans supported the first wave of the Black Lives Matter movement, which peaked after police killed Michael Brown in Ferguson in 2014.

Given that most Americans have a rather narrow understanding of racism, the juxtaposition of Black-led marches, meaning that racism was still present, and the inclusion of a Black family in the White House was undoubtedly perplexing to many at the time. Barack Obama's election was heralded as evidence that racism was on its way out.

Since the previous months of demonstrations were multiracial, the new, second wave of the uprising feels different. According to the media and academics, whites' sensibilities have been more attuned to anti-Black police brutality and injustice.

There was no systemic reform in response to Black Lives Matter activists' demands after the movement's first wave in 2014. Is it true that more white people are taking part in the latest demonstrations means the result will be different? Would whites endorse radical policy reforms to combat anti-Black racism and inequality in addition to marching?

I believe there are lessons from the 1960s civil rights movement that can help address those questions.

Policy did not develop from principles.

While the problems that Black Americans face today are not identical to those in the 1960s, the past is still important.

During the mid-twentieth-century civil rights movement, Black freedom fighters made a concerted attempt to show white Americans the types of racial terrorism the average Black American faced.

Whites were able to see firsthand how police viewed decent, peaceful Black teenagers as they pushed the United States to live up to its creed of liberty and equality for all of its people, thanks to the influence of media.

The Civil Rights Act and Voting Rights Act of 1964 and 1965, respectively, were landmark pieces of legislation, ostensibly providing freedom from racial discrimination in many public spaces as well as fair access to register to vote.

Furthermore, over the next few decades, whites were more likely to report views that many would now consider nonracist. White Americans, for example, were more open to having a black neighbor. They were less likely to believe in biological racism, or that white people should always have better jobs than black people.

However, these shifts in white ideals and views did not always translate into support for government policies that would offer racial equality to Blacks.

White Americans remained apathetic about school integration, which has been shown to significantly decrease the so-called "racial achievement gap Affirmative action policies" aimed at balancing the playing field in the workplace and higher education have never gotten more than a smattering of white support.

The principle "policy gap" is a term coined by social scientists to describe the gap between what people claim they believe and what they are willing to do to live up to those values.

The direct witnessing of police brutality by white Americans resulted in a change in racial views and the passage of landmark legislation. Even so, the face of racial injustice in American society has not changed dramatically due to these reforms.

Going Backwards

By the 1970s and 1980s, political figures had taken advantage of whites' perceptions that racial integration efforts had gone too far.

As a result, advances made during the civil rights movement were rolled back. Through the use of racial dog whistles, the Republican Party's so-called "Southern Strategy," which sought to convert white Southern Democrats into Republican supporters, was effective in gaining white Southerners' support. In addition, the War on Drugs will unfairly threaten, and police already segregated Black neighborhoods.

By the 1990s, racial inequalities in incarceration rates had skyrocketed, schools had begun to resegregate, and federal, and state policies that had generated residential segregation and exacerbated the racial wealth divide had never been adequately addressed.

What you should know

Scholars have worked to expose the complex and cultural nature of racism in the United States. Their findings range from demonstrating how racial inequalities in different aspects of American life are intricately related rather than coincidental, highlighting how race-neutral legislation like the GI Bill helped set the stage for today's racial wealth gap demonstrating that America's racial hierarchy is a caste structure.

However, research shows that white Americans, especially white millennials, have grown accustomed to thinking about racism in terms of overt racism, sexism, and bigotry. They are blind to the more complex issues that academics – and Black advocates – have identified.

As a result, much as it did for previous generations, it took a filmed incident of incendiary racism to awaken whites to the issues that Black activists had described as commonplace in the Black community.

Findings also indicate that people's perceptions of the issue affect their ability to support different policies. The fact that white Americans' perception of racism is too shallow to motivate them to endorse policies that may contribute to greater justice for Black Americans is a major problem that our society faces.

Chapter 6

The Rise And Effect Of Black Lives Matter

Black Lives Matter

Black Lives Matter (BLM) is an international social movement committed to combating racism and anti-Black violence, especially in the form of police brutality. It was founded in the United States in 2013. The name Black Lives Matter denotes both a criticism of unfair police shootings of Black people (Black people are much more likely to be murdered by cops in the United States than white people) and a demand that society respect Black people's lives and humanity as much as it values white people's lives and humanity.

BLM activists have staged massive, well-attended demonstrations in cities across the United States and around the world. Black Lives Matter is a decentralized grassroots movement led by leaders in local chapters who coordinate their own projects and services. The chapters are associated with the Black Lives Matter Global Network Foundation, a nonprofit civil rights organization that operates in the United States, Canada, and the United Kingdom.

Three Black community organizers— Opal Tometi, Alicia Garza, and Patrisse Khan-Cullors — cofounded BLM as an online campaign (using the hashtag #BlackLivesMatter on social media). Following the acquittal of George Zimmerman, a man of German and Peruvian origin, on charges linked to Trayvon Martin's fatal shooting, an unarmed Black teenager, in Sanford, Florida, in February 2012, they founded BLM. Zimmerman, a neighborhood watch volunteer, had seen Martin wandering around his neighborhood and reported him to the police because he seemed "suspicious." Despite police orders not to intervene, Zimmerman chased Martin, got into an argument with him, and shot him dead. Zimmerman was free for weeks after the shooting before being charged with second-degree murder and arrested in April, following nationwide protests calling for his indictment. Zimmerman pleaded self-defense at his sentencing, which took place more than a year later. His acquittal in July 2013 was generally seen as a miscarriage of justice, prompting further national demonstrations.

It was the Trayvon Martin murder that thrust attorney Benjamin Crump into the national spotlight. Contacted by Trayvon's father Tracy Martin, at first Crump was reluctant to take the case, presuming that Zimmerman would be arrested. "I believed in my heart of hearts that they were going to arrest him,"

Crump told the Associated Press a month later. He told Mr. Martin, "Oh they are going to arrest him. You don't need me on this." But as days went by with no arrest, Crump knew something was definitely wrong.

It was then that Crump contacted New York based civil rights leader Reverend Al Sharpton, who is the president of the National Action Network. Reverend Sharpton then reached out to me. As Senior Pastor of the Greater Friendship Baptist Church, the largest African American Baptist Church in Daytona Beach, we were only a stones throw away from the City of Sanford. At the time Rev. Sharpton contacted me, I was the 1st Vice Moderator of the Mount Zion Northeast Coast Baptist Association, as well as 5th Vice President of the Florida General Baptist Convention.

Together with local clergy from both Volusia and Seminole County I began to organize the first major rally to bring this tragic situation into the national spotlight. I immediately recognized that a local church in Sanford would not be large enough based on the social media responses we were seeing. Not only that but most major Black radio hosts, including Rev. Sharpton talked about the upcoming rally everyday.

Fortunately, I was able to work with the Mayor and City Manager in Sanford to identify a suitable location. After touring several potential locations, we settled on Fort Mellon Park in the historic district. Located on the shore of Lake Monroe it was an easy access off of Interstate Highway 4. The Sanford police and city staff were extremely cooperative in helping me. I could sense they wanted people to know that this murder was not representative of who the people of Sanford were.

The Trayvon Martin rally was a star-studded event, featuring Rev. Al; TV's Judge Mathis; radio personality Michael Baisden; NAACP President Ben Jealous; radio talk show host Joe Madison, and Marc Morial, CEO of the National Urban League, the nations largest civil rights organization. Even more surprising to me was how in just a few weeks time, a passion for justice for Trayvon, a previously unknown high school student, had spread not only nationally but internationally. People travelled from Hawaii, Australia, the U.K. and France to be in attendance. The police estimated the crowd to be in excess of 30,000. (Dr. L. Ronald Durham and this rally was written about by Lisa Bloom in her book Suspicion Nation).

After the police shootings of two unarmed Black men, Eric Garner and Michael Brown, the BLM movement grew in 2014. Garner died in New York after a white police officer put him in an unconstitutional chokehold for an extended period, caught on camera by a bystander. A white police officer gunned down Brown, a teenager in Ferguson, Missouri. Large demonstrations in the name of Black Lives Matter drew national and international attention to these deaths. Following that, the BLM campaign continued to play a leading role in anti-police violence and anti-racism protests. BLM activists, for example, protested the deaths of Sandra Bland, Philando Castile, Freddie Gray, Laquan McDonald, Tamir Rice, Walter Scott, Alton Sterling, and Breonna Taylor at the hands of police or while in police custody.

An unarmed Black man, George Floyd, was pronounced dead in 2020 after a white Minneapolis police officer named Derek Chauvin knelt for nine minutes and twenty nine seconds on Floyd's neck, ignoring Floyd's repeated cries that he couldn't breathe. The widespread distribution of a bystander's video of Floyd's last moments sparked huge protests in cities across the United States and worldwide. The tragedy swayed public opinion in the United States in favor of the Black Lives Matter movement while bringing widespread attention to institutionalized racism in the United States.

The Black Lives Matter campaign has several objectives. BLM activists aim to raise awareness of the many ways. Black people are treated differently in society and how institutions, rules, and policies contribute to that unfairness. Community activism, letter-writing campaigns, and peaceful marches have also been used by the movement to combat racism. BLM works to end police brutality, over-policing of minority communities, and crimes committed by for-profit prisons. Its initiatives also included calls for improved police training and increased responsibility for police misconduct. BLM advocates have also called for "defunding" the police, including cutting police budgets and reinvesting the savings in community social services like mental health and dispute resolution. BLM advocates have also worked in Black communities on voter registration and get-out-the-vote drives. Furthermore, Black Lives Matter campaigns have honored Black artists and writers.

The rise of Black Lives Matter: An attempt to Break the Cycle of Abuse and Silence

Critics predicted that it would not last. It was a minor blip on the protest radar. Like Occupy Wall Street, it will fade away. Some predicted it would fail because it lacked a clear structure and a strong leader, particularly once the infighting began. But it continues to grow – and polarize.

The Black Lives Matter campaign has repeatedly thrust itself into the national spotlight. Anyone seems to join them and claim to be a part of the movement simply by making a Facebook profile or using a hashtag.

Nonetheless, it is lauded as well as criticized. According to one of the co-founders, the group has branched out with branches in 31 cities and organized marches, boycotts, and other activities throughout the United States, even though it is impossible to know precisely how massive the movement has grown.

It has developed into a virtual juggernaut for a community that began with a hashtag in 2012 after the shooting death of Trayvon Martin in Florida. It has altered public perceptions of police brutality and racism.

"Thanks to social media, we can meet people in even the most remote parts of the United States. Patrisse Marie Cullors-Brignac, one of the co-founders of Black Lives Matter, says, "We're plucking at a cord that hasn't been plucked forever." "There is a hashtag and a network to rally around. Being in sync with our own people is extremely powerful."

You might try, but it's becoming increasingly difficult to avoid the topic of Black Lives Matter. That is precisely the point.

However, the organization is also struggling to find its feet to make even further progress. And part of that entails finding out what the movement is about in the long run, where leaders believe they should do more than demonstrate and disrupt society, or as they often chant, "shut sh*t down." They say it's about what it means to be black in America, not just about every actual death of an African American man or woman.

And that means learning how to effect political change to resolve the African American community's frustrations. The movement aims for a civil rights-style reform that shakes up politics and ends the cycle of violence and silence.

To do so, it must confront itself, its leadership, and how it intends to work. The lack of a prominent leader in the community is intentional.

Defending themselves against brutality and the path ahead

The Black Lives Matter movement is trying hard to avoid inciting crime. When it is accused of committing violent acts during marches, it retaliates vehemently. However, with a loosely organized community, this is to be anticipated. When you organize or promote demonstrations and encourage others to participate, the community and the campaign bear the brunt of the blame if any protesters become aggressive or destructive, as happened in Ferguson and Baltimore.

When activists in Minneapolis learned of a possible conspiracy by white nationalists to provoke violence to tarnish the movement, they took a different approach. They instructed group members to ensure that their faces were visible so that fingers could not be pointed at them.

When a man walking through the crowd was asked to remove his mask and declined, the group wondered why he was there in the first place. They grabbed his arm and escorted him out when he said he was just checking things out. Some people admired the group's behavior, while others criticized them. They were attempting to police themselves, but they also took someone off the street.

Threats towards the party are now coming in thick and heavy. The majority of them are accessible through the internet. However, others are available in person. Five protesters were shot in Minneapolis. After a clash between demonstrators and the men, police arrested three suspects, all of whom were white.

Despite the setbacks, roadblocks, and accusations, the movement continues to gain traction across the nation. The question is, what is the group's future plan, and will it have an effect on policy, or will it simply protest to make its presence known.

Effects of Black Lives Matter protests.

According to research, areas where BLM protests occurred between 2014 and 2019 saw a decline in police homicides but an increase in murders.

The impact of Black Lives Matter demonstrations on police use of lethal force has long been a source of heated discussion. According to a new report, the demonstrations have had a significant effect on police shootings, one of the first to make a systematic academic attempt to address that issue. Between 2014 and 2019, police killed one fewer person for every 4,000 people who attended a Black Lives Matter rally.

Travis Campbell, an economics Ph.D. student at the University of Massachusetts Amherst, published his preliminary results as a preprint on the Social Science Research Network, indicating that the analysis has not yet been peer-reviewed.

Although Campbell's study does not cover the events of summer 2020, George Floyd's assassination and the ensuing wave of demonstrations grew to become the largest movement in American history, fueled by a wave of outrage and grief over the police homicides that Americans are constantly exposed to on the television. Opinion columnists, advocates, lawmakers, and even the present and former presidents of the United States have weighed in on the demonstrations and suggested policy changes. But first, it's important to consider how the demonstrations have now influenced policing.

From 2014 to 2019, Campbell tracked nearly 350,000 people at over 1,600 BLM protests globally, mostly in larger cities. His key finding is that police officers used 15 to 20% less lethal force in census areas where BLM demonstrations occurred, resulting in about 300 fewer police killings.

According to his study, BLM protests are associated with a 10% rise in murders in the areas where they occur. That means that between 2014 and 2019, there were between 1,000 and 6,000 more homicides than would have been predicted if protesting areas followed the same pattern as non-protesting areas. Since researchers do not yet have all of the relevant data, Campbell's study excludes the results of last summer's historic wave of protests.

Since the murder results were not the main focus of Campbell's study, he did not expose them to the same battery of statistical measures as the police killings. (He plans to do further research into the impact of these protests on crime rates.) However, his homicide analysis is consistent with other facts. Given current protest studies, Omar Wasow, a professor at Princeton University who has done pioneering research on the impact of protests, told Vox that the findings are "entirely possible" and "not shocking."

The causes for the increase in murders are unknown, but one theory is that as a result of the scrutiny, police morale decreases, causing officers to decrease their efforts and thereby emboldening offenders. Another is that after a police homicide delegitimizes the justice system in their minds, public members willingly refrain from interactions with the police.

Protests have a lot of strength. They have the power to raise awareness, build solidarity or sever existing bonds, alter public opinion, reinforce or weaken institutions, and influence election outcomes. However, according to this report, BLM protests have the desired impact.

The effect of BLM demonstrations on police use of lethal force

The paper's main finding is that areas where BLM protests were held saw a statistically significant decrease in police homicides. Furthermore, when protests are massive and regular, the largest drops occur.

Campbell also observes that the disparity in police murder rates between areas with and without protests widens over time. He discovers a 13 percent decrease in police murders in year zero, which increases to 14 percentage points by year four. That means the impact of BLM protests is likely to be high enough to reduce the number of police homicides for many years.

Campbell argues that three mechanisms, none of which are mutually exclusive, may have contributed to the decline.

First, he saw a rise in the use of body cameras and various forms of community policing. Police forces likely introduced measures to eliminate lethal use of force in response to BLM demonstrations. According to the study, the possibility of an agency receiving body-worn cameras (55.3 percent), patrol officers within a given geographic area (20.6 percent), and SARA officers, a form of a community police officer, has increased significantly (57.5 percent).

However, the recent literature on body cameras is mixed, casting doubt on the notion that widespread body camera use is the sole cause of decreased police violence.

Although randomized trials "in American and European police departments found that body-worn cameras decreased the number of complaints lodged by residents against the police, they showed mixed results on the use of force by and against police officers," according to a Brookings Institution specialist. The researchers found that "the behavior of officers who wear cameras all the time was indistinguishable from the behavior of those who never wore cameras."

Taeho Kim, a University of Chicago economics researcher, discovered in a recent job market report that the use of body cameras reduced police-involved homicides by 43 percent around the world.

The research on other aspects of this potential interpretation is less obvious. While the effect of expanding community policing and patrols on lethal force is "understudied," activists have repeatedly called for community policing in the wake of police brutality.

It may not be the exact improvements per se, but the rise in institutional or preparation changes, according to Wasow, suggests that more people are taking responsibility seriously within the justice system. Since accountability culture is difficult to assess, researchers may look for signs of it in the rise of body-worn cameras and community policing. If this is the case, police reform may require greater dedication to keeping officers to a higher standard than specific policies.

The second mechanism is that, due to the demonstrations and the publicizing of police homicides, people are becoming more suspicious of the police. That may mean fewer people call 911 or speak with police officers on their own initiative, resulting in fewer civilian-police interactions and, as a result, fewer fatal incidents.

Finally, there's the Ferguson impact, which holds that demonstrations against police brutality lower officer morale and effort as a result of "intensified criticism from the community and media." In other words, officers become less violent in their work. This can result in fewer arrests, especially for less serious offenses such as disorderly conduct or marijuana possession.

Following officer-involved deaths, Deepak Premkumar, a research fellow at the Public Policy Institute of California, discovered in recently published research that police efforts are reduced: Arrests for theft are down 7%, and arrests for "quality of life offenses" like disorderly conduct or drug possession are reduced up to 23%. (Weed possession alone decreases by 33%).

These last two mechanisms could explain why there has been an uptick in murders since the BLM protests.

Is there a connection between BLM protests and an increase in homicides?

Things start to get a little more speculative at this point. According to the research, BLM protests are linked to a 10% rise in murder. Meaning, more murders in areas where BLM protests occurred than would have been predicted if those areas followed the same patterns as areas where protests did not occur.

We don't know why BLM protests are linked to a rise in homicides, and there isn't much study in this area to guide us. Furthermore, since the research query centered on the impact of BLM demonstrations on police homicides, these other reported shifts were not subjected to the same robustness measures.

The rise may be due to a variety of factors. According to Premkumar, who researched the Ferguson impact, there was a "major increase" (10 to 17 percent) in murders and robberies after high-profile officer-involved fatalities.

However, after speaking with experts, there are a few possibilities about what is going on here.

First, it's likely that illegal activity increases in places where demonstrations have occurred because citizens are afraid or angry, so they avoid calling the cops or cooperating with them, encouraging criminal conduct. Furthermore, some scholars suggest that if the system lacks credibility due to police homicide, people may attempt to settle their disputes outside of the legal system.

If this were to occur, we would expect to see a decrease in the overall rates of low-level crime, with fewer low-level crimes being reported in comparison to high-level crimes such as murders. Since there is a missing person and a corpse, homicides are less likely to go unnoticed. As a result, the murder rate is normally the best predictor of what's going on in general crime.

According to the study, there has been a substantial rise in the murder rate, but an 8.4% decline in overall property crimes registered. Some criminologists agree with this explanation, which is consistent with people actively minimizing encounters with the police. However, a study by a Ph.D. student at Harvard University found that "well-publicized violence events do not decrease 911 calls to report common property or violent crimes across a vast range of towns, incidents, and predictive strategies," casting doubt on the notion that police homicides reduce voluntary civilian involvement with the police.

Another reason for the increased murder rate is that law enforcement officers actively minimize their contact with the public, thus encouraging illegal activity. Observing if the share of property offenses cleared decreases over time is one way to see whether police are reducing their efforts. In other words, are the police not putting forth as much effort to solve low-level crimes that are reported to them, either because they are demoralized or upset at public criticism of their actions? Campbell notices a 5.5 percent drop in the number of property crimes cleared, which is consistent with police actions being scaled back immediately after the demonstrations.

The best part is that, even if Campbell's findings of a rise in murders after BLM protests are verified, the impact does not seem to last long. By year four, he no longer sees a statistically significant rise in murders, implying that whatever is causing the increase isn't likely to last.

None of his data includes the 2020 demonstrations or the increase in murders. "Some analysts have cited the demonstrations this summer over the police shootings of George Floyd and others," German Lopez writes for Vox, but Covid-19 made the year so unprecedented that experts are hesitant to draw any conclusions just yet.

Chapter 7

As Dr King Asked–Where Do We Go From Here?

Some have advocated for healing and progress. That sounds enticing, but let's not gloss over what's rotten under the surface. When democratic societies have been forced to confront atrocities, many have understood the value of exposing the truth in its entirety and keeping responsible parties accountable to the rule of law before any reconciliation can occur—from postwar

Germany to post-apartheid South Africa to post-Khmer Rouge Cambodia.

In this age of corrosive and deliberate disinformation, truth and the rule of law are particularly important. We've seen an onslaught of anti-democratic theories, discriminatory viewpoints, ludicrous conspiracies, and other negative narratives becoming more widely and profoundly accepted than ever before. To begin combating anarchy, our country's leaders must end the dissemination of lies and re-establish the rule of law, which is based on truth, integrity, and proof.

Dr. Martin Luther King Jr. often stressed the value of honesty in the pursuit of justice. He writes in Where Do We Go From Here: "It is time for all of us to tell each other the truth about who and what brought the Negro to the state of misery against which he struggles today." The reality is difficult to come by in human relations since most groups are misled about themselves. Psychological cataracts that blind us to our individual and collective sins are rationalization and the never-ending quest for scapegoats. Yet boring euphemisms have had their day. He who surrounds himself with lies is spiritually enslaved. Knowing the facts always comes with a bonus of freedom. "You shall know the truth, and the truth shall set you free," says the Bible."

Can we, as a nation, transcend our fractured belief systems, which have been hardened by lies, caricatured scapegoats, and strategic deception? I believe we can. I often look to today's spiritual leaders for inspiration, particularly those who have embraced Dr. King's call for "a true revolution of values." Dr. King's Poor People's Campaign is being revived in the twenty-first century, with the Rev. Dr. William J. Barber II calling for a "moral movement" to fight "the interlocking horrors of institutional injustice, poverty, ecological destruction, militarism, and the war economy, and the warped moral narrative of religious nationalism." The Rev. Dr. and Senator-Elect Raphael

Warnock affirms in a 2018 speech about Dr. King's "change of values" that such a revolution must be grounded in concrete steps—public policies, practices, and attitudes. He explains Dr. King "led the civil rights movement before the law became an instrument of emancipation" and that "he fought for the oppressed and died protecting workers—defending garbage collectors, fighting for their integrity, fighting for a living wage. "There is still a substantial amount of work to be completed."

"We still have an option today: nonviolent coexistence or violent coannihilation," Dr. King warns in the final passage. This may be humanity's last opportunity to choose between chaos and community." During these days between an insurgency and a presidential inauguration at the United States Capitol, I believe we not only have the option, but we must choose it every day since every day is Martin Luther King Jr. Day.

'How Do We Proceed From Here?' Amid the tumult of the 1960s, King's query still rings true today.

Martin Luther King, Jr., at a low point in his activist career, asked himself a question that was both important to the broader Civil Rights Movement and still relevant today: Where do we go from here?

King took a short break from the action, retreated to a villa in Jamaica, and wrote a book, appropriately titled "Where Do We Go From Here?" He was so torn about the condition of civil rights, the potential fracturing of the movement, and the tensions the Vietnam War was exerting on the nation that he took a brief break from the action, secluded himself in a villa in Jamaica and wrote a book, appropriately titled "Where Do We Go From Here"

It was June 1965, and there was no doubt that racial tensions were deteriorating. "Anyone who can look you in the eyes and assure you that Black America is in good shape is either lying or a fool," wrote Washington Post columnist William Raspberry. The movement, like the nation, was at a fork in the road. There was bickering, discussion, and disagreement back then, as there is now, on the best course of action.

There is a wide variety of feelings and viewpoints on the state of race relations, from those who think change is apparent to those who believe things are not as they seem. Those roles are represented by Courtland Cox and Clifford Alexander, Jr., two famous figures from the 1960s.

Alexander was a cornerstone in establishing influence in the struggle for integration when he served as chairman of the Equal Employment Opportunity Commission (EEOC) under President Lyndon B. Johnson and as the first Black Secretary of the Army under President Jimmy Carter. He is unhappy with current racial ties.

"Racism is on the rise now. "It's a lot worse than it used to be," he said. "There are more racists today who are simply unconcerned. They believe that Black people are useless. And the Trump administration has elevated prejudice in the eyes of the public."

Cox, a member of the Student Nonviolent Coordinating Committee (SNCC) when it took on Jim Crow in the Deep South's most segregated states, is upbeat about the future.

He expressed his optimism by saying, "Yes, there is more knowledge, more consciousness today, and that gives me hope." "The more diverse groups that participate, the better. Signs for Black Lives Matter are different now than they were in the 1960s, and that gives me hope."

"The change now is the level of hazard, it's a little lower now than in Mississippi," his SNCC colleague Judy Richardson said of the dangers Blacks faced in the South. Jennifer Lawson, another SNCC veteran, added that there is now a greater understanding of rights, with "a greater number of Blacks conscious of their rights and prepared to protect themselves."

Moderate groups, such as King's Southern Christian Leadership Conference, were heavily criticized at the time by college students and SNCC members. King and other leaders were accused by the youths of being out of step with the times and of being too friendly with whites, therefore too likely to go along to get along.

The debate is similar to the one currently underway between young Black Lives Matter activists and supporters and older establishment leaders. Race was a major issue back then, as it is now. Although the SCLC and other groups were strong supporters of integration, the SNCC youth had thrown whites out of the party.

When students at North Carolina A&T, an all-Black college in Greensboro, requested service at a whites-only lunch counter at Woolworth's Department Store, the slogan was "Black and white together" in 1960. Their actions sparked protests throughout the South, igniting the new Civil Rights Movement.

The irony of SNCC's conception and development is striking. SCLC leaders gave the young people a desk in the corner of their Auburn Avenue offices after the organization's establishment at Fisk University in Nashville, and the decision to establish headquarters in Atlanta. Ella Baker, SCLC's first executive director, urged the organization to help. Jane Stembridge and Ann Curry, two white students, ran the spontaneous activity from a corner desk before the new party relocated across the street. Atlanta served as the movement's de facto headquarters, just as London did during World War II's European era.

Despite the groups' mutual mistrust, the movement's sit-in period and subsequent protest activity were largely successful. Owing to civil rights legislation passed in 1964, 1965, and 1968, lunch counters were desegregated, putting an end to official Jim Crow in public places; previously denied jobs were opened to Blacks and other nonwhites, and many segregated communities were demolished.

After Stokely Carmichael, the SNCC leader from 1966 to 1967, raised a clenched fist and screamed, "Black Power," and said Blacks should break ties with whites, a schism formed among Black people. He was also the main reason behind the shift from the centuries-old labels of "colored" and "Negro" to African American and Black, which were once considered derogatory.

At first, those at the New York Times were unsure which word to use in their reporting. A. M. Rosenthal, the executive editor, eventually threw up his hands and told writers to use whatever word their sources desired. They did it for a while until Black and African Americans became the norm.

The 1970s and 1980s saw a dramatic change, with slow but steady improvement. More Blacks were elected to political office, the economy improved, and other ethnic groups made progress, and the general racial atmosphere improved.

In recent years, many more nonwhites and women have been elected to public office. The movement's current scope is also important. Demonstrations took place in every state during recent BLM protests. Furthermore, the number of white participants was higher than during the Civil Rights Movement.

Finally, President Joe Biden and Vice President Kamala Harris were elected, which is a positive sign. They've promised to make their administration more representative of America; if they succeed, there will be more nonwhites and women in the federal government than ever before.

What was King's answer to the issue of where we should go from here? "Never again will I be silent," he vowed. After returning to Atlanta from his Jamaican retreat, he focused his efforts on the war and the Poor People's Campaign. He promised to expand the coalition to include Mexican Americans, Puerto Ricans, Indians, and low-income whites.

He wrote, "Let us be those imaginative dissenters who will call our beloved nation to a higher destiny, a new plateau of compassion, a more noble expression of humaneness."

Do Not Go Yet; One Last Thing To Do

If you enjoyed this book or found it useful, I'd be very grateful if you'd post a short review on Amazon. Your support really does make a difference, and I read all the reviews personally so I can get your feedback and make this book even better.

Thanks again for your support!

Rev. Dr. L. Ronald Durham